LANGUAGE ARTS
INSTANT ASSESSMENTS
for Data Tracking

Grade 1

Credits
Content Editor: Jennifer B. Stith

Visit *carsondellosa.com* for correlations to Common Core, state, national, and Canadian provincial standards.

Carson-Dellosa Publishing, LLC
PO Box 35665
Greensboro, NC 27425 USA
carsondellosa.com

978-1-4838-3616-4
01-339161151

✦ Table of Contents ✦

© Carson-Dellosa • CD-104941

✦ Assessment and Data Tracking ✦

Data tracking is an essential element in modern classrooms. Teachers are often required to capture student learning through both formative and summative assessments. They then must use the results to guide teaching, remediation, and lesson planning and provide feedback to students, parents, and administrators. Because time is always at a premium in the classroom, it is vital that teachers have the assessments they need at their fingertips. The assessments need to be suited to the skill being assessed as well as adapted to the stage in the learning process. This is true for an informal checkup at the end of a lesson or a formal assessment at the end of a unit.

This book will provide the tools and assessments needed to determine your students' level of mastery throughout the school year. The assessments are both formal and informal and include a variety of formats—pretests and posttests, flash cards, prompt cards, traditional tests, and exit tickets. Often, there are several assessment options for a single skill or concept to allow you the greatest flexibility when assessing understanding. Simply select the assessment that best fits your needs, or use them all to create a comprehensive set of assessments for before, during, and after learning.

Incorporate Instant Assessments into your daily plans to streamline the data-tracking process and keep the focus on student mastery and growth.

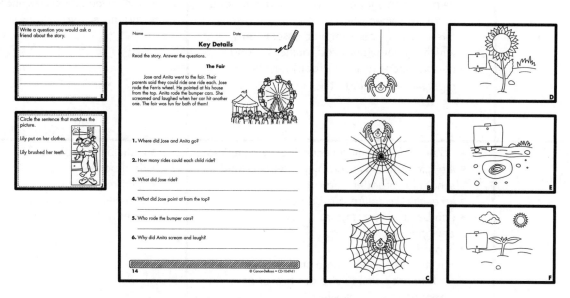

A variety of instant assessments for story elements

Types of Assessment

Assessment usually has a negative association because it brings to mind tedious pencil-and-paper tests and grading. However, it can take on many different forms and be a positive, integral part of the year. Not all assessments need to be formal, nor do they all need to be graded. Choose the type of assessment to use based on the information you need to gather. Then, you can decide if or how it should be graded.

	What Does It Look Like?	Examples
Formative Assessment	• occurs during learning • is administered frequently • is usually informal and not graded • identifies areas of improvement • provides immediate feedback so a student can make adjustments promptly, if needed • allows teachers to rethink strategies, lesson content, etc., based on current student performance • is process-focused • has the most impact on a student's performance	• in-class observations • exit tickets • reflections and journaling • homework • student-teacher conferences • student self-evaluations
Interim Assessment	• occurs occasionally • is more formal and usually graded • feedback is not immediate, though still fairly quick • helps teachers identify gaps in teaching and areas for remediation • often includes performance assessments, which are individualized, authentic, and performance-based in order to evaluate higher-level thinking skills	• in-class observations • exit tickets • reflections and journaling • homework • student-teacher conferences • student self-evaluations
Summative Assessment	• occurs once learning is considered complete • the information is used by the teacher and school for broader purposes • takes time to return a grade or score • can be used to compare a student's performance to others • is product-focused • has the least impact on a student's performance since there are few or no opportunities for retesting	• cumulative projects • final portfolios • quarterly testing • end-of-the-year testing • standardized testing

How to Use This Book

The assessments in this book follow a few different formats, depending on the skill or concept being assessed. Use the descriptions below to familiarize yourself with each unique format and get the most out of Instant Assessments all year long.

Show What You Know

Most anchors begin with two *Show What You Know* tests. They follow the same format with the same types of questions, so they can be used as a pretest and posttest that can be directly compared to show growth. Or, use one as a test at the end of a unit and use the second version as a retest for students after remediation.

Exit Tickets

Most anchors end with exit tickets that cover the variety of concepts within the anchor. Exit tickets are very targeted questions designed to assess understanding of specific skills, so they are ideal formative assessments to use at the end of a lesson. Exit tickets do not have space for student names, allowing teachers to gather information on the entire class without placing pressure on individual students. If desired, have students write their names or initials on the back of the tickets. Other uses for exit tickets include the following:

- Use the back of each ticket for longer answers, fuller explanations, or extension questions. If needed, students can staple them to larger sheets of paper.
- They can also be used for warm-ups or to find out what students know before a lesson.
- Use the generic exit tickets on pages 7 and 8 for any concept you want to assess. Be sure to fill in any blanks before copying.
- Laminate them and place them in a language arts center as task cards.
- Use them to play Scoot or a similar review game at the end of a unit.
- Choose several to create a targeted assessment for a skill or set of skills.

Word Lists

Word lists consist of several collections of grade-appropriate words in areas that students need to be assessed in, such as sight words, spelling patterns, and words with affixes. They are not comprehensive but are intended to make creating your own assessments simpler. Use the word lists to create vocabulary tests, word decoding fluency tests, spelling lists, etc., for the year.

Cards

Use the cards as prompts for one-on-one conferencing. Simply copy the cards, cut them apart, and follow the directions preceding each set of cards. Use the lettering to keep track of which cards a student has interacted with.

- Copy on card stock and/or laminate for durability.
- Punch holes in the top left corners and place the cards on a book ring to make them easily accessible.
- Copy the sets on different colors of paper to keep them easily separated or to distinguish different sections within a set of cards.
- Easily differentiate by using different amounts or levels of cards to assess a student.
- Write the answers on the backs of cards to create self-checking flash cards.
- Place them in a language arts center as task cards or matching activities.
- Use them to play Scoot or a similar review game at the end of a unit.

Assessment Pages

The reproducible assessment pages are intended for use as a standard test of a skill. Use them in conjunction with other types of assessment to get a full picture of a student's level of understanding. They can also be used for review or homework.

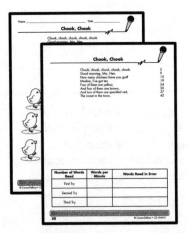

Fluency Pages

Use the paired fluency pages to assess students' oral reading fluency. Provide a copy of the student page to the student, and use the teacher copy to track how far the student read, which words he or she struggled with, and the student's performance on repeated readings. The word count is provided at the end of each line for easy totaling. Then, use the related comprehension questions to assess the student's understanding of what he or she read.

Exit Tickets

Exit tickets are a useful formative assessment tool that you can easily work into your day. You can choose to use a single exit ticket at the end of the day or at the end of each lesson. Simply choose a ticket below, and make one copy for each student. Then, have students complete the prompt and present them to you as their ticket out of the door. Use the student responses to gauge overall learning, create small remediation groups, or target areas for reteaching. A blank exit ticket is included on page 8 so you can create your own exit tickets as well.

What stuck with you today?

_____

_____

_____

_____

List three facts you learned today. Put them in order from most important to least important.

1. _____

2. _____

3. _____

The first thing I'll tell my family about today is

_____

_____

_____

_____ .

The most important thing I learned today is

_____

_____

_____

_____ .

Color the face that shows how you feel about understanding today's lesson.

Explain why. _____

_____

Summarize today's lesson in 10 words or less.

_____

_____

_____

_____

One example of _____ is _____

_____

_____

_____ .

One question I still have is _____

_____

_____

_____

_____ .

How will understanding _____

_____

help you in real life? _____

_____

_____

One new word I learned today is

_____ .

It means _____

_____

_____

_____ .

Draw a picture related to the lesson. Add a caption.

_____

_____

If today's lesson were a song, the title would be _____

_____

because _____

_____ .

The answer is _____ .

What is the question? _____

_____

_____

_____

Name _____ Date _____

✦ Show What You Know ✦
Reading: Literature

Read the story. Answer the questions.

My New Home

My family moves into a new home today. It is a yellow house. The house has a red door. The yard is big. It has many trees. I want to climb on them! I will be happy at my new home.

1. Draw a picture of the house.

2. Which words helped you color your picture?

yellow   tree   family   red

3. Who might be telling the story?

dog   boy   mother

4. What does the character want to do in the yard?

_____

5. How does the character feel about the new house?

sad   happy   mad

Show What You Know
Reading: Literature

Read the story. Answer the questions.

A Chilly Friend

It was a snowy day. Ethan and Hayden decided to make a snowman. They bundled up and ran outside. First, they rolled a great big snowball for the body. Then, they rolled a medium-sized snowball for the middle. Finally, they rolled a small snowball for the head. The boys stacked the snowballs. They found rocks for the eyes and the mouth. They used a carrot for the nose. They used sticks for the arms. The boys' mom came out of the house to admire their work. She brought a scarf, a hat, and mittens to add to the snowman. They stood back and admired their new chilly friend.

1. What kind of day was it?

_____

2. What did Ethan and Hayden decide to do?

_____

3. Number the events from the story in order.

_____ They rolled a medium-sized snowball.

_____ They found rocks for the eyes and the mouth.

_____ They rolled a great big snowball.

_____ They rolled a small snowball for the head.

_____ They stacked the snowballs.

4. Draw a picture of the snowman.

Story Elements

Use the story element cards to assess students' comprehension and retelling skills. Display a group of cards. Ask students to describe what they see on the cards. Have them place the cards in the order the story happens. Alternatively, display only cards that show characters (or settings or events) and have students tell a story about that character. If desired, laminate the cards for durability.

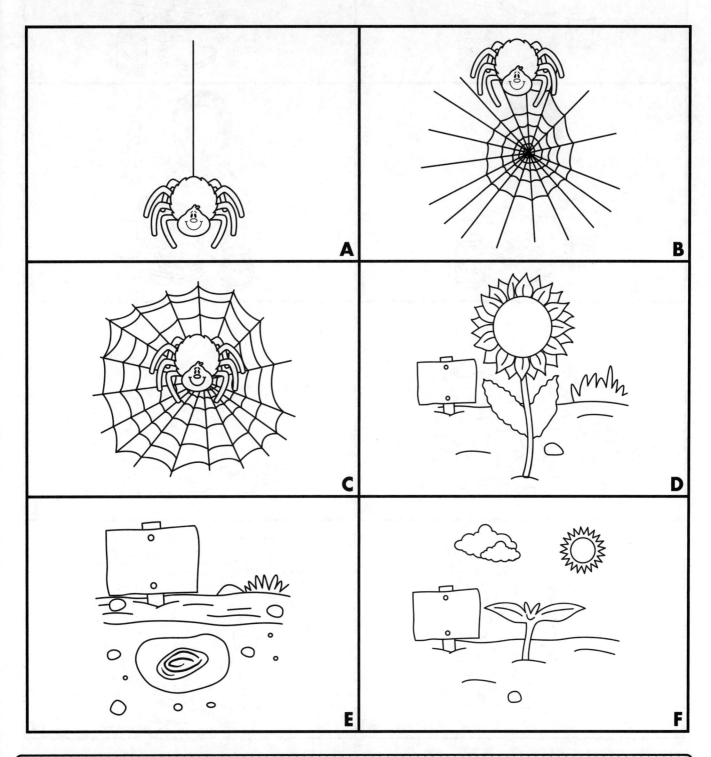

G

H

I

J

K

L

M

N

O

P

Q

R

S

T

U

V

Name _____ Date _____

Key Details

Read the story. Answer the questions.

The Fair

Jose and Anita went to the fair. Their parents said they could ride one ride each. Jose rode the Ferris wheel. He pointed at his house from the top. Anita rode the bumper cars. She screamed and laughed when her car hit another one. The fair was fun for both of them!

1. Where did Jose and Anita go?

_____

2. How many rides could each child ride?

_____

3. What did Jose ride?

_____

4. What did Jose point at from the top?

_____

5. Who rode the bumper cars?

_____

6. Why did Anita scream and laugh?

_____

Retelling a Story

Read the story. Draw a line through the sentences that are not part of the story.

The Three Little Pigs

The three little pigs leave their mother.

The first pig builds a house of straw.

Goldilocks sits in the three bears' chairs.

The wolf blows down the house of straw.

The second pig builds a house of sticks.

The wolf blows down the house of sticks.

Cinderella loses her glass slipper.

The third pig builds a house of bricks.

The wolf cannot blow down the house of bricks.

The turtle wins the race.

The wolf goes away.

The three little pigs live happily ever after.

Name _____ Date _____

Character and Setting

Read each story. Name the character(s) and the setting.

1. Katie lives on a farm. She takes care of horses. Katie wakes up early to open the barn. She feeds the horses and puts them in the stable. She fills their buckets with water. Then, she walks to school.

Character(s): _____

Setting: _____

2. Evan visits his grandmother. She lives in a special home because she is sick. Nurses take care of Evan's grandmother. When he visits, Evan eats lunch with his grandmother. Then, they play a game of cards.

Character(s): _____

Setting: _____

3. Nell's room was a mess! Her clothes were on the floor. Her shoes were on the desk. Nell even had a plate of old food under her bed. Her dad told her that it was time to do chores. Nell wanted to play outside instead. She could not go outside until her room was clean. Nell worked hard to clean up the mess. She was proud of herself when she looked at her tidy room.

Character(s): _____

Setting: _____

Name _____   Date _____

Events

Number the events in the order they happened.

1.

_____ Tanner's watch did not work in the morning.

_____ That evening, Tanner bought a new watch.

_____ At noon, Tanner tried to fix it.

2.

_____ Jack put two scoops of ice cream in the bowl.

_____ Jack got a bowl out of the cupboard.

_____ Jack put the empty bowl in the sink.

3.

_____ Nikki put on her raincoat.

_____ Nikki walked to the bus stop.

_____ Nikki watched the rain through the window.

4.

_____ Claire slid to the bottom.

_____ Claire ran to the slide.

_____ Claire climbed the ladder to the top.

Descriptive Language

Read the poem. Answer the questions.

In my flower garden, tulips always grow,
Straight like soldiers all in a row.

With colors so bright, reds, oranges, yellows too,
They are one of nature's special gifts just for you.

A tulip's colorful petals are shaped like a cup
Holding little raindrops for birds to drink up.

Winds cause them to sway
Back and forth each day.

But, still my tulips grow
Like soldiers in a row.

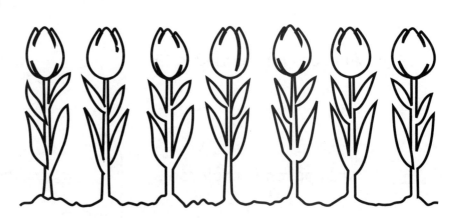

1. What is the poem about? Circle your answer.

a flower garden   tulips   soldiers

2. The author describes the tulips using other objects we know. Circle the objects the author used in the poem.

straight like soldiers

hard as a rock

shaped like a cup

nature's special gifts

3. Color the tulips with the colors the author describes.

Write what the story is about.

_____

_____

_____

_____

_____

A

Draw a character in the story.

B

Draw the setting of the story.

C

Write about one major event in the story.

_____

_____

_____

_____

_____

D

Write a question you would ask a friend about the story.

_____

_____

_____

_____

_____

E

Write about your favorite part of the story.

_____

_____

_____

_____

_____

F

Number the pictures in the order they would happen.

_____   _____   _____

G

Number the pictures in the order they would happen.

_____   _____   _____

H

Describe a kitten.

_____

_____

_____

_____

_____

_____

I

Circle the sentence that matches the picture.

Lily put on her clothes.

Lily brushed her teeth.

J

✦ Show What You Know ✦
Reading: Informational Text

There are many kinds of spiders. Spiders have eight legs. They like to eat insects. Many spiders spin webs. The web is a trap for small **prey**. The web is also a place for a spider to rest. Have you ever seen a spiderweb?

1. What is the text about?

        insects   spiders   legs

2. What do many spiders spin?

        yarn   strings   webs

3. What does the word **prey** mean?

        toys to play with   animals to eat

4. Use what you learned from the text to draw the spider's web.

Name _____   Date _____

Show What You Know
Reading: Informational Text

Alligators and Crocodiles

Alligators and crocodiles look and act very much the same. They are **cold-blooded**. They stay cool in the water and warm up in the sun. Alligators prefer to be in freshwater. Crocodiles are often found in salt water.

Both alligators and crocodiles are fierce hunters. They lie still in the water. But, they move fast to snap their long jaws on fish, birds, and other animals. An alligator's mouth is wide and round. You cannot see most of its teeth when its jaws are closed. A crocodile's mouth is pointy. You can see most of its teeth when its mouth is closed.

It is important to be careful near water. Stay back! An alligator or a crocodile may attack!

1. What is the main idea of this passage?

_____

_____

2. List some things that are the same and different about alligators and crocodiles.

_____

_____

_____

3. Write the sentence that helps you understand the meaning of **cold-blooded**.

_____

_____

4. Draw a picture of each animal's mouth. Label the pictures.

Name _____   Date _____

Key Details

Read the paragraph. Answer the questions.

     A fox can live in the woods, near a farm, or in the desert. Foxes can even live in the city. They run fast. They hunt for what they eat. They can have red, gray, or white fur. A baby fox is called a kit. A fox's home is called a den.

1. Name two places a fox can live.

_____   _____

2. What colors of fur can foxes have?

_____   _____   _____

3. How do foxes get food? _____

4. What is a fox's home called? _____

Main Idea

Read the text.

Lightning

The sky lights up with a flash. Crash! Thunder booms. Lightning is a very big electric spark. Thunder is the noise made by lightning.

Lightning happens during a storm. The dark clouds fill with a charge. The electricity in the clouds moves very fast to the ground. The path of the electricity is a bright streak of light. It is called lightning.

Lightning moves faster than its sound. When lightning is close, you hear the thunder at the same time. When lightning is far away, the thunder booms later. When you see lightning, count the seconds until the thunder. If you count five seconds, the lightning is one mile (1.6 km) away. If you count 10 seconds, the lightning is two miles (3.2 km) away.

Answer the questions with complete sentences. Gather information from books and the computer to help you. Share your information with a friend.

1. What is the main idea of this text?

_____

_____

2. Write a sentence that tells about the main idea.

_____

_____

3. Write one question you have about lightning.

_____

_____

Connecting Information

Whose Job Is It?

In the plains of Africa, a pride of lions lives together. A beautiful male lion walks around his family. He roars and scares other lions away. The female lions take care of the cubs. They play and stay together.

When a herd of zebras runs nearby, the female lions hunt. The females run fast and catch food for the pride.

The lions work together to keep their home and find food.

Use the phrases from the Job Bank to complete the chart.

Job Bank

hunts	keeps other lions away
	takes care of cubs

Who does each job?

Male Lion	Female Lion

Name _____ Date _____

New Words

Use the text to help you find out the meaning of each word.

Monarch Butterfly Life Cycle

A monarch butterfly goes through many changes in its short life. An adult butterfly lays one egg on a milkweed leaf. The egg hatches into a **larva**. The small caterpillar eats leaves. It grows bigger. The caterpillar is soon ready to change. It forms a green sack around its body. The caterpillar will stay in a **chrysalis** for a few weeks. Then, the sack opens. The caterpillar is now a butterfly. Then, the **life cycle** starts again.

1. Write the words from the text that helped you find out the meaning of the word **larva**.

_____

_____

2. Write the words from the text that helped you find out the meaning of the word **chrysalis**.

_____

_____

3. What is a **life cycle**? How do you know?

_____

_____

4. Circle the picture that shows a chrysalis.

 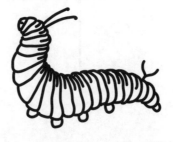 

Name _____ Date _____

Text Features

Use the table of contents to answer the questions.

Table of Contents

1. The title of Chapter 2 is _____.

2. Chapter _____ begins on page 15.

3. How many chapters are in the book? _____

4. Chapter _____ would tell you about brown bats.

5. Bats have a thumb on each wing. Chapter _____ would tell you this fact.

6. Chapter _____ will tell you what bats eat.

7. Chapter 4 begins on page _____ .

Text and Pictures

Read the text. Look at the pictures. Draw a line to match each text to the picture it describes.

Troy plays by a pond. There are ducks swimming in the pond. Many trees grow near the pond.

Kristen lives on a farm. A fence is in front of her house. A barn is near her house.

Peter lives in a tall building. There is a park near the building. People can walk their dogs in the park.

Author's Purpose

Read the text. Answer the questions.

Dinosaurs

Dinosaurs were big, but they looked and acted like birds. Dinosaurs had hollow bones just like birds do. We all know that birds hatch from eggs. Now, we know that dinosaurs hatched from eggs too. Scientists found some very old nests with eggs that had turned to stone. The nests were far, far apart. A mother that was 23 feet (7 m) long could lie on her nest to keep the eggs warm without touching another nest. Dinosaur mothers took care of their babies until they could walk. Bird mothers take care of their babies until they can fly. Scientists think that dinosaurs were just like birds. Maybe birds are just small dinosaurs.

1. What was the author's purpose for writing this text? Circle your answer.

to persuade

to inform

to entertain

2. List three ways the author says that dinosaurs and birds are alike.

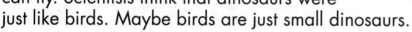

_____

_____

_____

3. Write the sentence that shows the author's opinion or thoughts.

_____

_____

Name _____ Date _____

Compare and Contrast

Read the texts. Answer the questions.

Ants at Work

Ants work hard. They work together. Each ant has a different job. Some ants get food. Some ants carry sand. Ants are strong. The queen has many babies. Other ants take care of the baby ants. Ants are hard workers.

Ants

Ants are insects. They have three body parts—the abdomen, the thorax, and the head. Ants also have six legs. They have two antennae. Some ants are black and some are red. Some ants are big and some ants are small.

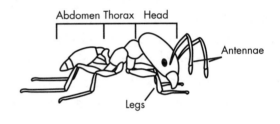

1. What is the main idea of **Ants at Work**?

_____

_____

2. What is the main idea of **Ants**?

_____

_____

3. How are the two paragraphs the same? How are they different?

_____

_____

4. Write one question you still have about ants.

_____

_____

Write two facts you learned from the text.

_____

_____

_____

_____

A

Draw a picture of something you learned in the text.

B

What is the main idea of the story?

_____

_____

_____

_____

_____

_____

C

Think about something you learned from the text. Describe how it connects to something you know or just learned from a different text.

_____

_____

_____

_____

_____

D

Write a new word you learned from the text.

_____

What does it mean?

_____

_____

_____

E

Use a word you learned from the text in a sentence.

_____

_____

_____

_____

_____

F

Find a book. Complete the title page.

_____
(title)

by

_____

Illustrated by

_____

G

Look at the Table of Contents. Answer the question.

What chapter might tell you how big a

baby bear is? _____

H

Circle the reason an author might have for writing about each topic.

Snails

to persuade   to inform   to entertain

Dental Health

to persuade   to inform   to entertain

Making Ice Cream

to persuade   to inform   to entertain

I

Write one topic you could write about that would inform a reader. List three facts you would include.

_____

_____

_____

_____

_____

_____

J

Complete the Venn diagram with details from two different texts about the same topic.

K

Describe your favorite part of the book.

_____

_____

_____

_____

_____

_____

L

Name _____   Date _____

✦ Show What You Know ✦
Reading: Foundational Skills

Say the name of each picture. Circle the pictures in each row whose names have the same vowel sound.

1.

2.

3.

4.

Say the name of each picture. Circle the pictures in each row whose names have the same beginning sounds.

5.

6.

7.

8.

Say the name of each picture. Circle the digraph you hear in both words.

9.   ch   sh   th   wh

10.    ch   sh   th   wh

11.    ch   sh   th   wh

12.    ch   sh   th   wh

Read each word. Write an **e** at the end of each word. Say the new word.

13. not_____

14. cut_____

Draw a line to divide each word into its syllables. Write the number of vowel sounds you hear.

15. a   i   r   p   o   r   t   _____

16. g   a   r   d   e   n   _____

17. f   u   n   n   y   _____

18. p   e   n   c   i   l   _____

Name _____ Date _____

Show What You Know
Reading: Foundational Skills

Say the name of each picture. Circle the pictures in each row whose names have the same vowel sound.

1.

2.

3.

4.

Say the name of each picture. Circle the pictures in each row whose names have the same beginning sounds.

5.

6.

7.

8.

Say the name of each picture. Circle the digraph you hear in both words.

9.    ch   sh   th   wh

10.   ch   sh   th   wh

11.    ch   sh   th   wh

12.   ch   sh   th   wh

Read each word. Write an **e** at the end of each word. Say the new word.

13. hop_____

14. pin_____

Draw a line to divide each word into its syllables. Write the number of vowel sounds you hear.

15. p i l l o w   _____

16. t i g e r   _____

17. b u t t e r   _____

18. c h i p m u n k   _____

Print Concepts

Use the key to circle the text on the page.

red	=	letter
blue	=	word
brown	=	sentence

I go to school.   saw

me

A   G   z

You are nice.   We eat pizza.

m   cat

go   R
                         d
went

Z   P   X

                              I love puppies.

I am seven.
                    they   r

Print Concepts

Read each sentence.

Draw a green ● where you would start reading.

Draw a red ● where you would stop reading.

Circle the capital letters.

Underline all ending punctuation.

Henry and his dog take a walk every day.

All plants need sun and rain to grow.

A spider spins a web to catch her food.

Are you going to the game?

Seaweed can be used to make ice cream!

I saw bears, tigers, and zebras at the zoo.

I missed the bus this morning!

Can you go to the mall with me?

Phonemes/Letter Sounds

Use these cards to assess and reinforce beginning, middle, and ending letter sounds. Display a small group of cards and say a letter sound (beginning, middle, or end). Have a student point to the card that has that sound in the correct position. Alternatively, display one card at a time. Have the student say the name of the picture. Then, have him say another word that has the same beginning, middle, or ending sound as the picture. If desired, laminate the cards for durability so that a student can use write-on/wipe-away markers to write the word on the back of a picture.

A

B

C

D

E

F

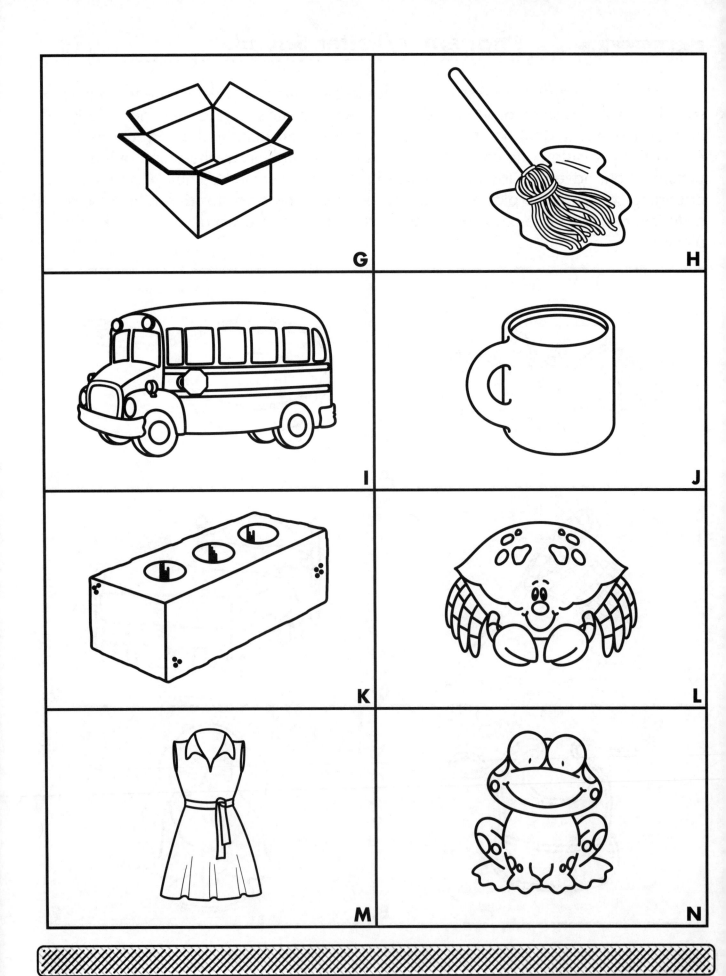

G

H

I

J

K

L

M

N

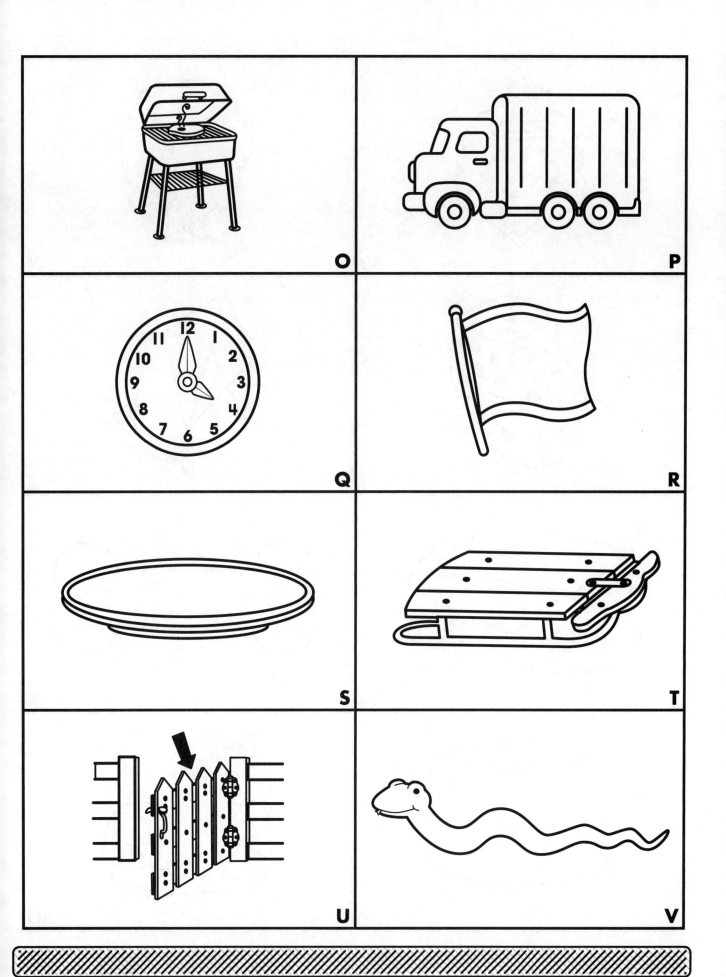

O

P

Q

R

S

T

U

V

W

X

Y

Z

AA

AB

AC

AD

Name _____   Date _____

Short Vowel Sounds

Say the name of each picture. Write the missing letter for each short vowel sound.

1. w _____ g

2. c _____ p

3.  b _____ t

4.  l _____ g

5. p _____ n

6.  h _____ t

7. f _____ n

8.  r _____ g

9. m _____ p

10. b _____ d

Say the name of each picture. Circle the pictures in each row whose names have the same short vowel sound.

11.

12.

13.

14.

15.

Name _____ Date _____

Long Vowel Sounds

Say the name of each picture. Circle the pictures in each row whose names have the same long vowel sound.

1.

2.

3.

4.

5.

Say the name of each picture. Circle the letter of the long vowel sound you hear in each word.

6.

a e i o u   a e i o u   a e i o u

7.

a e i o u   a e i o u   a e i o u

8.

a e i o u   a e i o u   a e i o u

Short and Long Vowel Sounds

Say the name of each picture. Circle the vowel sound in each word.

1.

short u

long u

2.

short i

long i

3.

short e

long e

4.

short a

long a

5.

short o

long o

6.

short i

long i

7.

short a

long a

8.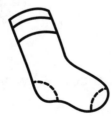

short o

long o

9.

short e

long e

Blending Sounds

Say the name of the first picture in each row. Circle the picture whose name has the same beginning sound.

1.

2.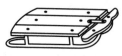

3.

4.

5.

6.

Say the name of each picture. Circle the correct word.

7.

clown

crown

8.

glue

blue

9.

stump

slump

Blending Sounds

Say the name of each picture. Circle the letters of the beginning sounds.

1.

st   sp

2.

dr   tr

3.

cr   cl

4.

fr   fl

5.

sl   pl

6.

dr   gr

7.

cr   gr

8.
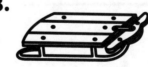

sl   st

9.

br   bl

10.

sw   tw

Beginning, Middle, and Ending Sounds

Say the name of each picture. Write the letter of the missing beginning, middle, or ending sound.

1.  an

2.  do

3.  t p

4.  ig

5.  ar

6. 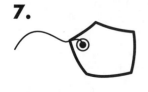 gu

7. 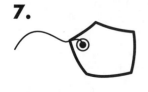 ta

8. 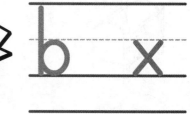 b x

9.  s n

10.  p n

Digraphs

Say the name of each picture. Write the missing letters in each word.

1.  __ick

2. 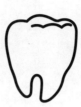 too__

3.  pea__

4. __ale

5.  __eese

6. __orn

7.  __eep

8.  __eat

9. fi__

10. bran__

Silent *E* Words

Read each word. Write an **e** at the end of each word. Draw a line to match each word to the picture it names.

1. can_____

2. pin_____

3. pip_____

4. tap_____

5. kit_____

6. cap_____

7. not_____

8. Tell or write what happens to the vowel sound when a silent **e** is put at the end of each word.

_____

_____

Counting Syllables

Say each word. Write the number of syllables you hear. Write the number of vowel sounds you hear.

Word	Syllables	Vowel Sounds
1. bus		
2. rabbit		
3. truck		
4. jumping		
5. window		
6. three		
7. running		
8. butter		
9. school		
10. carrot		
11. brick		
12. doghouse		

13. Tell or write why the number of syllables is the same as the number of vowel sounds in each word.

_____

_____

Dividing Syllables

Say each word. Draw a line to divide each word into its syllables. Write a rule for each set of words.

---

wallet	butter	zipper	yellow
sister	pretzel	doctor	purple
summer	hammer	garden	donkey

_____

_____

---

robot	baby	open	human
cable	police	paper	baker
pilot	tiger	silent	clover

_____

_____

---

popcorn	fishbowl	pancake	rainbow
bathtub	sandbox	bookcase	airport
raincoat	handbag	shoelace	starfish

_____

_____

Word Lists

Use these lists of words when you are assessing language concepts. The lists are not comprehensive but can be used as grade-level examples for creating your own assessments, flash cards, etc.

Short Vowels

Words with Short A
- bag
- bat
- can
- cat
- fan
- hat
- map
- mat
- tag
- van

Words with Short E
- bed
- gem
- hen
- leg
- men
- pen
- red
- ten
- vet
- web

Words with Short I
- bib
- dig
- fin
- hip
- lid
- lip
- pin
- six
- wig

Words with Short O
- box
- cob
- cot
- dot
- fox
- log
- mop
- top

Words with Short U
- bun
- bus
- cub
- cup
- hut
- mug
- nut
- pup
- sun
- tub

Long Vowels

Words with Long A
- cake
- lake
- page
- vase
- mail
- rain
- sail
- day
- ray

Words with Long E
- bee
- feet
- seed
- bead
- bean
- leaf
- seal
- seat
- tea

Words with Long I
- bike
- dime
- hive
- ice
- kite
- mice
- mine
- pipe
- rice
- fly
- sky
- pie
- tie

Words with Long O
- bone
- cone
- hose
- nose
- pole
- rope
- rose
- coat
- loaf
- soap
- row
- doe
- toe

Words with Long U
- blue*
- bugle
- cube
- cute
- glue*
- mule
- music
- ruler*
- tube*
- unicorn

*These words have the /oo/ sound instead of the /yoo/ sound.

Word Lists

R-Blends
braid
branch
bread
brick
broom
brush
crab
crane
crib
crow
crown
drain
dress
drill
drip
drum
grape
graph
grass
green
grill
pretzel
prince
princess
prize
prune
track
trail
train
tray
tree
truck

L-Blends
black
blanket
block
blouse
blue
clam
clay
clip
cloud
clown
club
flag
flame
flower
flute
glass
globe
glove
glue
plane
plate
plug
plum
sled
slide
slipper
slug

S-Blends
scale
scarf
scoop
scooter
skate
ski
skull
skunk
smile
smoke
snail
snake
snow
star
stem
step
stool
stop
stove
swan
swim
swing

Digraphs
Ch
chain
chair
cheese
cherry
chick
chin
bench
branch
inch
peach

Sh
shape
shark
sheep
shell
ship
shirt
shoe
shovel
brush
bush
dish
fish
leash

Th
thirty
thorn
thumb
bath
math
path
teeth
tooth
wreath

Wh
whale
wheat
wheel
whistle

Name _____   Date _____

Bailey at the Park

My dog, Bailey, loves to go to the park. Every Saturday morning, I take Bailey to the park to play. The first thing Bailey does is run down to the pond. Bailey likes to splash in the water. She does not mind the cold water. When she gets out of the water, she shakes and shakes. I stand back so that she does not get me wet. Then, she finds a sunny spot in the grass. She takes a nap. I read a book. When it is time to go home, I whistle for her to come. I think our Saturday trips to the park are something Bailey looks forward to all week.

Bailey at the Park

My dog, Bailey, loves to go to the park. Every Saturday morning, I   13

take Bailey to the park to play. The first thing Bailey does is run down to the   30

pond. Bailey likes to splash in the water. She does not mind the cold water.   45

When she gets out of the water, she shakes and shakes. I stand back so   60

that she does not get me wet. Then, she finds a sunny spot in the grass. She   77

takes a nap. I read a book. When it is time to go home, I whistle for her   95

to come. I think our Saturday trips to the park are something Bailey looks   109

forward to all week.   113

Number of Words Read	Words per Minute	Words Read in Error
First Try		
Second Try		
Third Try		

Chook, Chook

Chook, chook, chook, chook, chook.
Good morning, Mrs. Hen.
How many chickens have you got?
Madam, I've got ten.
Four of them are yellow,
And four of them are brown,
And two of them are speckled red,
The nicest in the town.

Chook, Chook

Chook, chook, chook, chook, chook.	5
Good morning, Mrs. Hen.	9
How many chickens have you got?	15
Madam, I've got ten.	19
Four of them are yellow,	24
And four of them are brown,	30
And two of them are speckled red,	37
The nicest in the town.	42

Number of Words Read	Words per Minute	Words Read in Error
First Try		
Second Try		
Third Try		

Fluency Comprehension Questions

Bailey at the Park (pages 55 and 56)

1. Who is Bailey?

2. What are some things that Bailey likes to do at the park?

3. What does the narrator say about how Bailey feels about their trips to the park?

Chook, Chook (pages 57 and 58)

1. How many chicks does Mrs. Hen have?

2. Describe Mrs. Hen's chicks.

Word Lists

Use these lists of words when you are assessing language concepts. The lists are not comprehensive but can be used as grade-level examples for creating your own assessments, flash cards, etc.

Sight Words		Number Words
after	live	zero
again	may	one
an	of	two
any	old	three
as	once	four
ask	open	five
by	over	six
could	put	seven
every	round	eight
fly	some	nine
from	stop	ten
give	take	**Color Words**
giving	thank	red
had	them	orange
has	then	yellow
her	think	green
him	walk	blue
his	were	purple
how	when	brown
just		black
know		white
let		gray

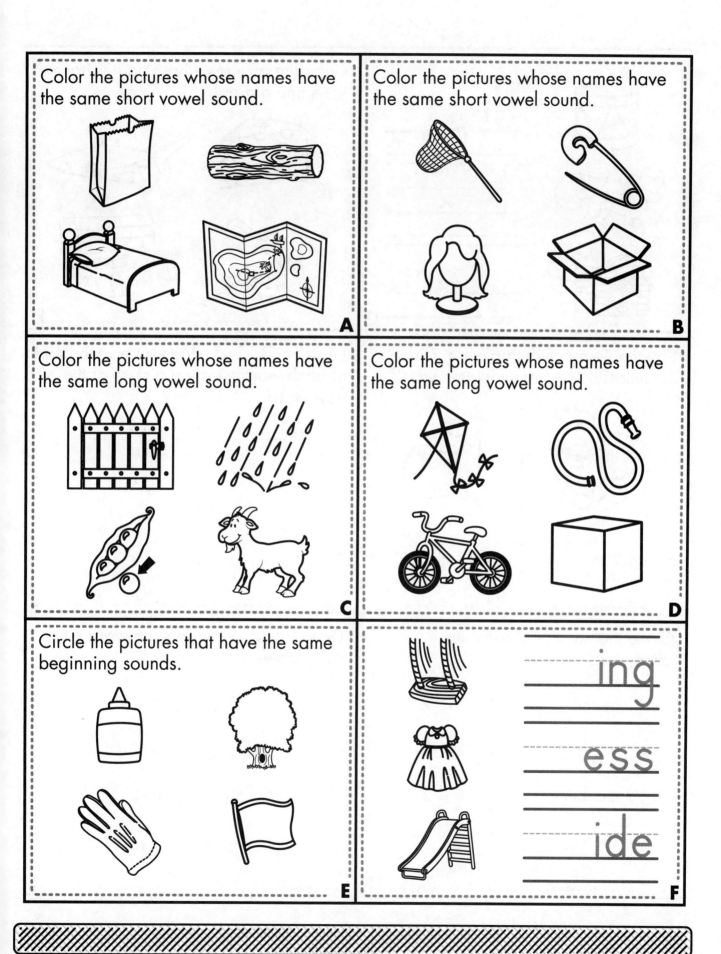

Color the pictures whose names have the same short vowel sound.

A

Color the pictures whose names have the same short vowel sound.

B

Color the pictures whose names have the same long vowel sound.

C

Color the pictures whose names have the same long vowel sound.

D

Circle the pictures that have the same beginning sounds.

E

ing

ess

ide

F

G
dru___
f_x
___arn

H
Color the pictures whose names have the same digraph.

I
Say the name of each picture. Circle the letters of the beginning sound.

ch   th   sh   th   wh   sh

J
Read each word. Write an **e** at the end of each word. Draw a picture of the new word.

can_____   kit_____

K
Circle the number of syllables in each word.

queen	1	2
garden	1	2
teacher	1	2
shoe	1	2

L
Draw a line to divide each word into its syllables.

p e p p e r

d o g h o u s e

s i l e n t

d o c t o r

Name _____ Date _____

Writing an Opinion Piece

Draw a picture of a pet you have or would like to have.

Is it hard to take care of a pet? Why or why not? Explain your opinion with at least three sentences.

_____

_____

_____

_____

_____

_____

_____

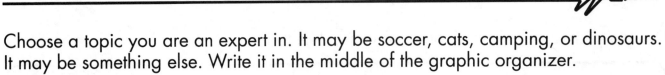

Writing an Informational Text

Choose a topic you are an expert in. It may be soccer, cats, camping, or dinosaurs. It may be something else. Write it in the middle of the graphic organizer.

Complete the graphic organizer. Write about your topic.

Writing a Narrative

Draw a picture in the oval of what you want to do when you grow up. Finish the story.

When I grow up, I want to be a

_____

because . . .

_____

_____

_____

_____

_____

_____

_____

_____

_____

Writing a Sequence of Events

Write the steps for making an ice-cream sundae. Use the pictures to help you.

_____

_____

_____

_____

_____

_____

_____

_____

_____

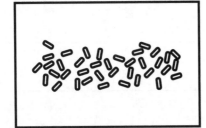

_____

_____

_____

_____

_____

_____

What is your favorite toy? Why?

_____

_____

_____

_____

_____

A

Do you like to sleep with the light on or off? Explain.

_____

_____

_____

_____

_____

B

Do you think you should have to learn to read? Why or why not?

_____

_____

_____

_____

_____

_____

C

Write about a topic you know a lot about.

_____

_____

_____

_____

_____

_____

D

Explain how to do something that you already know.

_____

_____

_____

_____

_____

E

Write a question you have about

_____.

_____

_____

_____

_____

F

Write the first sentence to a story about

a _____.

_____

_____

_____

_____

G

Write the last sentence to a story about

a _____.

_____

_____

_____

_____

H

Write one detail you would include in a

story about _____.

_____

_____

_____

_____

I

Write about a time you felt happy.

_____

_____

_____

_____

_____

J

Write the steps to washing your hands.

_____

_____

_____

_____

_____

_____

K

Write the steps to brushing your teeth.

_____

_____

_____

_____

_____

_____

L

Show What You Know
Language: Conventions

1. Match each uppercase letter to its lowercase letter.

N	e
D	n
E	d
B	k
K	r
R	b

2. Circle the nouns in each sentence.

The computer has a screen, keyboard, and mouse.

Squirrels and birds live in trees.

3. Underline the verbs in each sentence.

Ms. Lee told us a story about dragons.

Susie runs around the track many times.

4. Circle the adjectives in each sentence.

The large truck dropped off a heavy box.

Mr. Wong uses a red pen to grade his papers.

5. Write the ending punctuation for each sentence.

May I play outside ☐

I like to eat yogurt for a snack ☐

What is your name ☐

6. Write the missing commas in the sentence.

Matt and Joe carry bags of eggs bread and milk to the car.

Show What You Know
Language: Conventions

1. Match each uppercase letter to its lowercase letter.

V	g
G	y
L	h
Y	u
H	v
U	l

2. Circle the nouns in each sentence.

The car has a frame, body, engine, and wheels.

Whales and sharks live in oceans.

3. Underline the verbs in each sentence.

Mr. Lopez called my mom on the phone.

Goats will eat grass and even paper.

4. Circle the adjectives in each sentence.

The little mouse ate the yellow cheese.

The man delivers many envelopes and large boxes.

5. Write the ending punctuation for each sentence.

Math is my favorite subject ☐

Can you tie a bow ☐

Look out for the puddle ☐

6. Write the missing commas in the sentence.

Your keys coins and pen fell out of the hole in your pocket.

Forming Letters

Trace the letters. Then, write each uppercase and lowercase letter.

Aa

Bb

Cc

Dd

Ee

Ff

Gg

Hh

Ii

Jj

Kk

Ll

Mm

Nn

Oo

Pp

Qq

Rr

Ss

Tt

Uu

Vv

Ww

Xx

Yy

Zz

Parts of Speech

Use the key to circle the text on the page.

> red = nouns
> blue = verbs
> brown = adjectives

pen

girl

loud

loud

sleeps

frog

car

pond

runs

green

hops

talks

eats

hard

cold

Common and Proper Nouns

Circle the nouns in each sentence. Make the first noun in each sentence plural.

1. The horse jumped over the fence. _____

2. The boy will walk to school. _____

3. The clam is under the sand. _____

4. A bear sleeps in winter. _____

5. The gold key opens the door. _____

Circle the proper noun. Rewrite it correctly.

6.   my friend   megan   _____

7.   mr. walsh   my teacher   _____

8.   my street   arbor drive   _____

9.   dr. woods   my dentist   _____

10.   my state   utah   _____

Write a proper noun for each underlined noun.

11. The girl ran in to the water. _____

12. The teacher read a book. _____

13. We went to the city to see the parade. _____

14. The doctor listened to my heart. _____

Possessive Nouns and Pronouns

Draw lines to match each noun to a pronoun.

1. Grant   she

2. Nana and I   they

3. Miss Long   we

4. car   he

5. Molly and Jon   it

Circle the word that could replace the underlined word or words in each sentence.

6. <u>Paul's</u> shoe is lost again.

       Her   His

7. Do not forget to call <u>Mom's</u> phone!

       her   his

8. <u>Mary and Kate's</u> room is very tidy.

       Her   Their

9. <u>The bear's</u> cubs are learning to hunt.

       Its   His

10. Where are <u>Ginny's</u> toys?

       her   their

Verb Tenses

Underline the verb in each sentence. Then, write the past tense of the verb.

1. Tom smells the pie in the oven. _____

2. Mia climbs up the ladder. _____

3. The frogs hop on the rock. _____

4. Grandma helps me with the cake. _____

5. The man pulls the fire hose. _____

Circle the verb form that best completes each sentence.

6. Dad _____ the school tomorrow.

        called   call   will call

7. The cat _____ from the shelf while I watched.

        jumped   jumps   will jump

8. Whales _____ to each other using many sounds.

        talked   talk   will talk

9. The baby just _____ over to the toy.

        crawled   crawls   will crawl

10. They _____ the game yesterday.

        watched   watch   will watch

Write a sentence using the past, present, and future tense of the verb *march*.

11. past tense: _____

_____

12. present tense: _____

_____

13. future tense: _____

_____

Adjectives

1. Circle the words that can be used describe an apple.

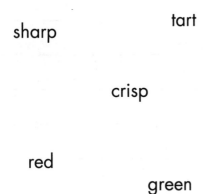

sharp

tart

soft

sweet

crisp

black

red

green

round

Circle the adjective in each sentence.

2. The loud trucks go down the street.

3. A brown toad hops on a leaf.

4. The bird eats a small bug.

5. My cat is furry.

6. Her fancy dress is on the hook.

Use each adjective in a sentence.

7. bumpy _____

_____

8. stinky _____

_____

9. yellow _____

_____

10. shiny _____

_____

Sentences

Rewrite each sentence correctly.

1. i am so scared

_____

2. how old are you

_____

3. they rode the bus home

_____

4. that was so much fun

_____

5. our teacher read us a book

_____

6. where are you going

_____

7. jeff likes to use a computer

_____

8. my favorite food is pizza

_____

9. when will we go to the store

_____

10. insects have three body parts

_____

Commas

Add the missing commas in each sentence.

1. Make sure you pack socks shoes and a hat for our hike.

2. Jeff saw lions cheetahs and jaguars at the zoo.

3. We bought bananas tomatoes and onions at the market.

4. Brandon jumped crawled and wiggled his way through the obstacle course.

5. Lidia Joanne and Marin made beaded bracelets.

6. You will need eggs flour and butter to make waffles.

7. Grandpa read me books about space oceans and rocks.

8. Beth plays piano flute and trumpet in music class.

9. Connor Sam and Gwen are good friends.

10. Please tell me your name address and phone number.

A

Circle the nouns.

A tree grows in our backyard.

My pencil broke during the test.

B

Circle the verbs.

Could you please put my book on the shelf?

Do not eat so fast!

C

Circle the correct verb tense.

will run   past   present   future

jumped   past   present   future

helps   past   present   future

D

Underline the proper nouns.

Mr. Jordan and Dad mowed their lawns today.

Someday I want to travel to Spain and Italy.

E

Write the pronoun that replaces each word or words.

Alex and Ben   the door

_____   _____

Miss Diaz   Mom and I

_____   _____

F

Circle the correct pronoun to replace the underlined words in each sentence.

Dez's tooth is loose.

          Her   Your

The bird's nest is in the bush.

          Their   Its

My dad and mom's car is red.

          His   Their

Circle the adjectives.

big house

tiny hole

fuzzy bunny

three bears

G

Write an adjective to describe each noun.

_____ puppy

_____ cloud

_____ man

_____ truck

H

Add commas in each sentence.

She walks to school on Mondays Wednesdays and Fridays.

Henry Sam and Ty are going to the movies.

We saw lobsters sharks and eels in the large tank.

I

Circle the word that should be capitalized. Write the correct ending punctuation.

what an awesome goal____

the girl picked the yellow dress____

J

Circle the word that should be capitalized. Write the correct ending punctuation.

how many animals did you see____

the horses walked through the gate____

K

Add the correct punctuation to each sentence.

Rob saw starfish clams and fish in the tide pool

Don't forget to pack your toothbrush pillow and pajamas

L

80

✦ Show What You Know ✦
Language: Vocabulary

Circle the meaning of each underlined nonsense word.

1. Please clean up your <u>yegz</u>!

        food   mess   car

2. Join us for Tim's <u>rinple</u> party.

        sleeping   running   birthday

Add the prefix **un-** or **re-** to each word. Write the meaning of the new word.

3. _____tie means _____.

4. _____write means _____.

Add the suffix **-er** or **-ful** to each word. Write the meaning of the new word.

5. Fear_____ means _____.

6. Play_____ means _____.

Cross out the word that does not belong in each category.

7. Colors	**8. Vegetables**	**9. Toys**
yellow	lettuce	car
blue	bread	doll
rain	carrot	pillow
red	cucumber	game

Circle the words in each row that have almost the same meaning.

10.   eat   chew   drive   swallow

11.   whisper   yell   shout   exclaim

✦ Show What You Know ✦
Language: Vocabulary

Circle the meaning of each underlined nonsense word.

1. Drive to the <u>trypa</u> and buy some milk.

school   store   house

2. Let's play a board <u>brod</u>!

game   sock   dog

Add the prefix **un-** or **re-** to each word. Write the meaning of the new word.

3. _____happy means _____.

4. _____heat means _____.

Add the suffix **-er** or **-ful** to each word. Write the meaning of the new word.

5. Help_____ means _____.

6. Hope_____ means _____.

Cross out the word that does not belong in each category.

7. Shoes	**8. Fruit**	**9. Fish**
boot	desk	trout
pencil	pear	wolf
sandal	banana	tuna
sneaker	orange	shark

Circle the words in each row that have almost the same meaning.

10.   scared   sad   frightened   afraid

11.   happy   cheerful   joyful   perfect

Inflectional Endings

Circle the word that correctly completes each sentence.

1. One day, Wendy, Will, and their father decided to go (camp, camping, camped).

2. They (pack, packing, packed) everything that they would need on their bikes.

3. Then, off they rode to (hunt, hunting, hunted) for a good place to camp.

4. Finally, after looking for a long time, they (pick, picking, picked) a great campsite.

5. (Park, Parking, Parked) their bikes was tricky because it was very muddy.

6. Wendy lost control and went (splash, splashing, splashed) into a pond.

7. Will ran over and quickly (pull, pulling, pulled) Wendy out.

8. Wendy's shoes were (fill, filling, filled) with water and even a small fish.

9. After that, they all sat on a rock to (rest, resting, rested).

10. Then, they (help, helping, helped) each other put up a tent.

Name _____ Date _____

Context Clues

Circle the meaning of the underlined nonsense word. Highlight the word or words in the sentence that helped you.

1. I use <u>xapt</u> to clean.

fast

soap

time

2. The <u>zoto</u> hopped in the grass.

rabbit

doll

car

3. We planted <u>kibd</u> in the garden.

ducks

boys

seeds

4. There is a <u>cefl</u> in the sky.

door

cloud

tree

5. We rode our <u>huvot</u> to the park.

bikes

house

ball

6. You must <u>japc</u> your room.

jump

sleep

clean

7. She went to a birthday <u>leehm</u>.

party

bath

plant

8. The cat is <u>niacp</u> the chair.

sing

blow

under

Name _____ Date _____

Prefixes

Add the prefix **un-** to each word. Write the meaning of one of the new words.

1. _____like

2. _____load

3. _____lock

4. _____done

5. _____ means _____.

Add the prefix **re-** to each word. Write the meaning of one of the new words.

6. _____read

7. _____view

8. _____play

9. _____tell

10. _____ means _____.

Suffixes

Add the suffix **-er** to each word. Write the meaning of one of the new words.

1. paint_____

2. teach_____

3. sing_____

4. play_____

5. _____ means _____.

Add the suffix **-ful** to each word. Write the meaning of one of the new words.

6. help_____

7. care_____

8. hope_____

9. play_____

10. _____ means _____.

Categorizing Words

Draw a line through the word that does not belong in each list.

1. Farm Animals

cow

hen

lion

pig

2. Kitchen Tools

spoon

knife

crayon

pan

3. Insects

ant

snake

ladybug

bee

4. School Tools

glue

drill

crayon

paper

5. Sports

soccer

reading

ballet

tennis

6. Ocean Animals

camel

shark

whale

crab

7. Clothing

sock

broom

pants

shirt

8. Foods

pizza

apple

chalk

bread

9. Family

mother

doctor

brother

uncle

10. Bedroom

desk

oven

closet

bed

11. Vehicles

house

truck

car

bus

12. Zoo Animals

tiger

bear

hamster

zebra

Shades of Meaning

Color the words in each row that have almost the same meaning.

1.	mad	angry	glad	cross
2.	awful	amusing	funny	silly
3.	hop	leap	sleep	jump
4.	small	good	little	tiny
5.	sad	pretty	beautiful	lovely
6.	run	sprint	teeny	jog
7.	big	large	fancy	huge

Choose a set of words from above. Use each word in a sentence to show that you understand their shades of meaning.

8. _____

_____

_____

9. _____

_____

_____

10. _____

_____

_____

A

The word _____ means

_____

_____

_____

_____

_____

_____ .

B

Use the word _____ in a sentence.

_____

_____

_____

_____

_____

_____

C

Write the words from the sentence that helped you know the meaning of

_____ .

_____

_____

_____

_____

_____

_____

D

Add the prefix **un-** or **re-** to each word. Write the meaning of one of the words.

_____heat   _____like

_____sure   _____read

_____ means _____

_____

_____ .

E

Add the suffix **-er** or **-ful** to each word. Write the meaning of one of the words.

farm_____   thank_____

sing_____   care_____

_____ means_____

_____

_____ .

F

Rewrite the base words with each ending.

	-s	-ed	-ing
work			
laugh			
start			

Match each word to its category.

hammer   cat

dog   **Pets**   drill

fish   **Tools**   wrench

saw   hamster

G

Write five words that fit in the category

of _____.

_____

_____

_____

_____

H

Rewrite each sentence correctly.

she puts on her green rain boots

_____

_____

when do we leave for the party

_____

_____

I

Rewrite each sentence correctly.

that is an amazing trick

_____

_____

aunt lisa is a nurse at my school

_____

_____

J

Circle the words that have almost the
same meaning.

glance   stare

climb   talk

look

watch

peer

K

Circle the words that have almost the
same meaning.

small   tiny

green   teeny

little

huge   bumpy

L

Answer Key

Page 9
1. Answers will vary. 2. yellow, red, (tree if yard is included in drawing); 3. boy; 4. The child wants to climb the trees. 5. happy

Page 10
1. It was a snowy day. 2. The boys decided to build a snowman. 3. The order is 2, 5, 1, 3, 4. 4. Answers will vary.

Page 14
1. Jose and Anita went to the fair.
2. They could each ride one ride. 3. Jose rode the Ferris wheel. 4. He pointed at his house from the top. 5. Anita rode the bumper cars. 6. Anita screamed and laughed when her car hit another one.

Page 15
Students should draw a line through *Goldilocks sits in the three bears' chairs*, *Cinderella loses her glass slipper*, and *The turtle wins the race*.

Page 16
1. Katie is a girl. She lives on a farm.
2. Evan is a boy who has a sick grandmother. His grandmother lives in a special home. 3. Nell is a girl. She has a messy room.

Page 17
1. 1, 3, 2; 2. 2, 1, 3; 3. 2, 3, 1; 4. 3, 1, 2

Page 18
1. tulips; 2. straight like soldiers, shaped like a cup, nature's special gifts; 3. Students should color the tulips red, orange, and yellow.

Pages 19–20
A–F. Answers will vary. G. 2, 3, 1; H. 2, 1, 3; I. Answers will vary. J. Lily put on her clothes.

Page 21
1. spiders; 2. webs; 3. animals to eat; 4. Check students' work.

Page 22
1. Alligators and crocodile are similar animals that have different features.
2. Alligators and crocodiles both live in water. Alligators and crocodiles are cold-blooded. Alligators prefer freshwater. Crocodiles are found in salt water. Alligators have round mouths that show little teeth when closed. Crocodiles have pointy mouths that do show teeth when closed. 3. They stay cool in the water and warm up in the sun. 4. Check students' work.

Page 23
1. woods, desert, farm, or city; 2. red, gray, white; 3. Foxes hunt for their food. 4. A fox's home is called a den.

Page 24
1. Lightning is part of a storm.
2. Lightning happens during a storm.
3. Answers will vary.

Answer Key

Page 25
Male lion: keeps other lions away;
Female lion: hunts, takes care of cubs

Page 26
1–2. Answers will vary. 3. the changes
an animal goes through during its life;
Answers will vary. 4. Students should
circle the third picture.

Page 27
1. Where Bats Live; 2. 5; 3. 5; 4. 1;
5. 4; 6. 3; 7. 12

Page 28
Check students' work.

Page 29
1. to inform; 2. They both have hollow
bones. They both hatched from eggs.
Dinosaur mothers stayed close to their
nests. 3. Maybe birds are just small
dinosaurs.

Page 30
1. Ants work hard. 2. to describe an
ant's appearance; 3. Both paragraphs
give information about ants. The first
tells about ants' behavior. The second
paragraph tells about how ants look.
4. Answers will vary.

Pages 31–32
A–G. Answers will vary. H. 4; I. to
inform, to persuade/to inform, to inform;
J–L. Answers will vary.

Pages 33–34
1. hose, goat, bowl; 2. bus, sun, mug;
3. mop, fox, pot; 4. knee, feet, teeth;
5. frame, frog, fruit; 6. stop, stool, star;
7. plug, plate, plant; 8. clown, clock,
cloud; 9. ch; 10. wh; 11. sh; 12. th;
13. note; 14. cute; 15. air/port (2);
16. gar/den (2); 17. fun/ny (2);
18. pen/cil (2)

Pages 35–36
1. pen, net, bed; 2. van, map, cat;
3. cake, rain, hay; 4. soap, goat, nose;
5. drum, dress, drill; 6. glass, glue,
glove; 7. brick, brain, bread; 8. snake,
snail, snow; 9. sh; 10. ch; 11. th;
12. sh; 13. hope; 14. pine; 15. pil/low
(2); 16. ti/ger (2); 17. but/ter (2);
18. chip/munk (2)

Page 37–38
Check students' work.

Page 43
1. i; 2. u; 3. a; 4. o; 5. i; 6. a; 7. a;
8. u; 9. o; 10. e; 11. hen, jet, bed;
12. pan, mat, cap; 13. wig, pin, fish;
14. bus, sun, gum; 15. mop, fox, pot

Page 44
1. chain, gate, hay; 2. globe, phone,
rope; 3. bike, dice, pie; 4. bee, peach,
cheese; 5. glue, mule; 6. e, o, u; 7. i, o,
a; 8. i, a, o

Page 45
1. short u; 2. long i; 3. short e; 4. short
a; 5. long o; 6. short i; 7. long a;
8. short o; 9. long e

Answer Key

Page 46
1. tray; 2. sled; 3. plant; 4. frame;
5. crib; 6. clown; 7. crown; 8. glue;
9. stump

Page 47
1. st; 2. dr; 3. cl; 4. fl; 5. pl; 6. gr;
7. cr; 8. sl; 9. br; 10. sw

Page 48
1. f; 2. g; 3. o; 4. w; 5. j; 6. m; 7. g;
8. o; 9. u; 10. i

Page 49
1. ch; 2. th; 3. ch; 4. wh; 5. ch; 6. th;
7. sh; 8. wh; 9. sh; 10. ch

Page 50
1. cane; 2. pine; 3. pipe; 4. tape;
5. kite; 6. cape; 7. note; 8. Answers
will vary.

Page 51
1. 1, 1; 2. 2, 2; 3. 1, 1; 4. 2, 2; 5. 2,
2; 6. 1, 1; 7. 2, 2; 8. 2, 2; 9. 1, 1;
10. 2, 2; 11. 1, 1; 12. 2, 2;
13. Answers will vary.

Page 52
The words in the first section should be
divided between the middle consonants.
The words in the second section should
be divided after the first vowel (long
vowel). The words in the third section
should be divided between the two
smaller words in each compound word.

Page 59
Bailey at the Park: 1. Bailey is a dog.
2. play in the water, take a nap in the
sun; 3. Bailey looks forward to them.
Chook, Chook: 1. 10; 2. yellow, brown,
speckled red

Pages 61–62
A. bag, map; B. pin, wig; C. gate, rain;
D. kite, bike; E. glue, glove; F. sw, dr, sl;
G. m, o, b; H. cheese, chain, bench;
I. sh, wh; J. cane, kite; K. 1, 2, 2, 1;
L. pep/per, dog/house, si/lent, doc/tor

Pages 63–65
Answers will vary.

Page 66
Answers will vary, but text should match
each picture.

Pages 67–68
A–L. Answers will vary.

Page 69
1. Check students' work. 2. computer,
screen, keyboard, mouse, Squirrels,
birds, trees; 3. told, runs; 4. large,
heavy, red; 5. ?, ., ?; 6. eggs, bread,
and milk

Page 70
1. Check students' work. 2. car, frame,
body, engine, wheels, whales, sharks,
oceans; 3. called, will eat; 4. little,
yellow, many, large; 5. ., ?, !; 6. keys,
coins, and pen

Answer Key

Page 71–72
Check students' work.

Page 73
1. horse, fence, horses; 2. boy, school, boys; 3. clam, sand, clams; 4. bear, bears; key, door, keys; 6. Megan; 7. Mr. Walsh; 8. Arbor Drive; 9. Dr. Woods; 10. Utah; 11–14. Answers will vary.

Page 74
1. Grant/he; 2. Nana and I/we; 3. Miss Long/she; 4. car/it; 5. Molly and Jon/they; 6. His; 7. her; 8. Their; 9. Its; 10. her

Page 75
1. smells, smelled; 2. climbs, climbed; 3. hop, hopped; 4. helps, helped; 5. pulls, pulled; 6. will call; 7. jumped; 8. talk; 9. crawled; 10. watched; 11–13. Answers will vary.

Page 76
1. Answers will vary but could include round, red, sweet, tart, green, and crisp. 2. loud; 3. brown; 4. small; 5. furry; 6. fancy; 7–10. Answers will vary.

Page 77
1. I am so scared! 2. How old are you? 3. They rode the bus home. 4. That was so much fun! 5. Our teacher read us a book. 6. Where are you going? 7. Jeff likes to use a computer. 8. My favorite food is pizza. 9. When will we go to the store? 10. Insects have three body parts.

Page 78
1. Make sure you pack socks, shoes, and a hat for our hike. 2. Jeff saw lions, cheetahs, and jaguars at the zoo. 3. We bought bananas, tomatoes, and onions at the market. 4. Brandon jumped, crawled, and wiggled his way through the obstacle course. 5. Lidia, Joanne, and Marin made beaded bracelets. 6. You will need eggs, flour, and butter to make waffles. 7. Grandpa read me books about space, oceans, and rocks. 8. Beth plays piano, flute, and trumpet in music class. 9. Connor, Sam, and Gwen are good friends. 10. Please tell me your name, address, and phone number.

Pages 79–80
A. tree, backyard, pencil, test; B. put, do eat; C. future, past, present; D. Mr. Jordan, Dad, Spain, Italy; E. they, it, she, we; F. Her, Its, Their; G. big, tiny, fuzzy, three; H. Answers will vary. I. She walks to school on Mondays, Wednesdays, and Fridays. Henry, Sam, and Ty are going to the movies. We saw lobsters, sharks, and eels in the large tank. J. What, !; The, .; K. How, ?; The, .; L. Rob saw starfish, clams, and fish in the tide pool. Don't forget to pack your toothbrush, pillow, and pajamas!

Page 81
1. mess; 2. birthday; 3. Untie means to not tie. 4. Rewrite means to write again. 5. Fearful means full of fear. 6. Player means someone who plays. 7. rain; 8. bread; 9. pillow; 10. eat, chew, swallow; 11. yell, shout, exclaim

Answer Key

Page 82
1. store; 2. game; 3. Unhappy means not happy. 4. Reheat means to heat again. 5. Helper means someone who helps. 6. Hopeful means full of hope. 7. pencil; 8. desk; 9. wolf; 10. scared frightened, afraid; 11. happy, cheerful, joyful

Page 83
1. camping; 2. packed; 3. hunt; 4. picked; 5. Parking; 6. splashing; 7. pulled; 8. filled; 9. rest; 10. helped

Page 84
1. soap; 2. rabbit; 3. seeds; 4. cloud; 5. bikes; 6. clean; 7. party; 8. under

Page 85
1. unlike; 2. unload; 3. unlock; 4. undone; 5. Answers will vary. 6. reread; 7. review; 8. replay; 9. retell; 10. Answers will vary.

Page 86
1. painter; 2. teacher; 3. singer; 4. player; 5. Answers will vary. 6. helpful; 7. careful; 8. hopeful; 9. playful; 10. Answers will vary.

Page 87
1. lion; 2. crayon; 3. snake; 4. drill; 5. reading; 6. camel; 7. broom; 8. chalk; 9. doctor; 10. oven; 11. house; 12. hamster

Page 88
1. mad, angry, cross; 2. amusing, funny, silly; 3. hop, leap, jump; 4. small, little, tiny; 5. pretty, beautiful, lovely; 6. run sprint, jog; 7. big, large, huge; 8–10. Answers will vary.

Pages 89–90
A–C. Answers will vary. D. reheat, unlike, unsure, reread, Answers will vary. E. farmer, thankful, singer, careful, Answers will vary. F. works, worked, working; laughs, laughed, laughing; starts, started, starting; G. Pets: dog, fish, cat, hamster; Tools: hammer, saw, wrench, drill; H. Answers will vary. I. She puts on her green rain boots. When do we leave for the party? J. That is an amazing trick! Aunt Lisa is a nurse at my school. K. look, stare, glance, peer, watch; L. small, little, tiny, teeny

Notes